Knitting
The 4-Hour Crash Course
To Knitting Like A
Pro

By Reshma Balkaran

Table of Contents

Introduction

Thank you and congratulations on purchasing *Knitting: The 4-Hour Crash Course To Knitting Like A Pro;* the book that will give you everything you need to begin knitting like a pro quickly and simply.

For me, knitting was always more of an art than just a needlecraft skill. There are so many knitting techniques that have been developed over the many years it has existed, creating more and more possibilities in what you can create!

Of course, like any other art form, you need to learn the basics before the advanced. The same way we learn how to brush paint on canvas before we can paint a picture, you'll need to learn how to put stitches on your knitting needles before you knit your first masterpiece!

The great news is, contrary to popular belief, there are really only a few steps you need to learn to begin knitting. In fact, all knitting is essentially made up of two basic stitching methods, the Knit Stitch and the Purl Stitch. Eventually you will be able to learn all the advanced knitting methods and patterns involving these two stitches to create different textures in your knitting. In this book you'll learn some basic stitch patterns involving the Knit stitch and the Purl stitch.

This book breaks down all the steps from getting your first stitches on the needle, how to create the two basic stitches, create stitch patterns, and binding off your first knitted piece. You will also learn some knitting terms and techniques to be able knit from a knitting pattern.

There is a satisfying feeling knowing that you have made something with your own hands. Creating your own articles gives you a chance to really explore your imagination. Have fun picking out different coloured yarn with different textures, and really find the style that reflects your own personality. It makes every piece you create uniquely your's. Take pride and joy knowing that you can wear or show off something that is your very own creation!

Chapter 1

Materials

Knitting Needles

Once you really start to get into knitting you can start to invest in more tools, but if you are just beginning to knit remember to keep it basic and simple. Really all you will need to get through the basics to knitting is a pair of single pointed straight needles and some yarn!

Straight (Single Pointed) Knitting Needles

Single pointed needles are one of the most popular kind of knitting needle used for knitting flat projects like scarves or blankets. They are straight needles with one pointed end, and one capped end so that stitches will not fall off the back. *I recommend a pair of straight knitting needles to begin your knitting journey, and no smaller than US size 8 needles. (See Needle Sizes and Conversions Chart on Page 10)*

Double Pointed Needles

Double pointed needles usually come in sets of four or five. They are straight needles with two pointed ends. When knitting with double pointed needles, you are usually knitting with four or five needles at once. This type of knitting is called **circular knitting** or **knitting in the round** used to create tube-like knitting articles like socks and mittens.

Circular Knitting Needles

Circular knitting needles are great because it can be used to create circular knitting or flat knitting. Circular needles are two straight needles that are connected together by a cord usually made by material like nylon so that it can hold its shape. In circular knitting, all the stitches are connected together in a circle around the cord.

Crochet Hooks

Although we won't be covering crocheting in this book, it is always good to know what a Crochet hook looks like, because it can actually be really helpful in knitting to fix mistakes. A crochet needle is a straight needle with one hooked end and can be made of metal, wood, plastic, or bone.

Other Knitting Tools

Cable Stitch Needles

Cable needles either look like small straight, double pointed needles or small double pointed needles with a curved centre. Their purpose is to create cable stitches which add texture to the knitting piece and give a sort of "twisted rope" look.

Stitch Markers

Stitch markers are great to have handy when you are knitting any projects. These markers are small rings that you can place on your needle when you need to mark a spot in your knitting.

Stitch Holders

Stitches are placed on a stitch holder so that the needle can be removed without the stitches unravelling.

Blunt Pointed Tapestry Needles

Tapestry needles look like sewing needles except that they are larger and the eye of the needle is big enough to thread your yarn. This is used to sew knitted pieces together. They can also be used to weave in the ends or tails of your knitted pieces.

Needle Sizes and Conversions

Knitting Needles come in many different sizes, and choosing the size of needle for your knitting can be confusing because different regions have their own knitting needle sizes.

US needle sizes are used most commonly in North American regions. Each knitting needle is sized according to the thickness of the needle. The thinner the needle is, the smaller the size number will be. The thicker the needle the bigger the size number will be.

UK needle sizes are more popular in the Eastern regions of the world and are similar to the US size system in that they are sized by the thickness of the needle. However, size numbers range the opposite way than US sizes. The thinner the knitting needle, the bigger the size number will be and the thicker the knitting needle the smaller the size number will be.

The metric size is usually written on the needle next to the US or UK size. Both US sizes and UK sizes can be converted to the metric sizes. Use a needle conversion chart to find out what size needle a pattern is requiring. which is the diameter of the needle measured in millimeters.

Needle Conversion Chart

Metric (mm)	US	UK
2.0	0	14
2.25	1	13
2.75	2	12
3.0	-	11
3.25	3	10
3.5	4	-
3.75	5	9
4.0	6	8
4.5	7	7
5.0	8	6
5.5	9	5
6.0	10	4
6.5	10 1/2	3
7.0	-	2
7.5	-	1
8.0	11	0
9.0	13	00
10.0	15	000
12.0	17	-
16.0	19	-
19.0	35	-
25.0	50	-

Yarn

Choosing the yarn for your project is the most exciting part of knitting! There are so many different types of yarn and so many different colors to choose from, you may want to walk into the store and buy them all! Yarn is made from so many different materials like various plant fibers, animal furs, and many synthetic fibers. The colors can vary from very vibrant and bright hues to more subtle, pastel hues.

Animal Fibre	Plant Fibre	Synthetic Fibre
Wool	Cotton	Acrylic
Alpaca	Flax	Nylon
Angora	Hemp	Polyester
Beaver	Bamboo	Aramids
Cashmere (goat)	Corn	Basofil
Fox	Rayon	Spandex
Rabit		Polyethelene
Possom		Sulfar
Camel		
Vicuna		
Buffalo		
Silk		

Organic Yarns

Organic yarns are a great choice if you would like to choose a yarn that has a lesser impact on the planet. Organic yarns are those that have not been processed through chemicals and the upbringing of the yarn sources have been untouched and grown completely natural.

Organic animal fiber is considered organic due to the lack of growth hormones the animal will have and will be fed organic and natural food. The process of the wool after it is removed from the sheep is chemical free.

Organic Plant fibers are considered organic because it is grown without using any fertilizers or pesticides to promote growth. Hemp is a plant material that is naturally organic because it grows so easily and quickly it does not require any added pesticides.

Yarn Weight

Yarn is classified by the thickness of the yarn called the yarn weight. The yarn thickness can depend either on how many fiber strands the yarn contains or how thick the yarn strands are. In order to categorize different yarn weights, all the types of yarn are standardized by the *Craft Yarn Council of America,* and each category of yarn can be found on the **Standard Yarn Weight Chart.**

The Standard Yarn Weight Chart

Standard Yarn Weight System
Categories of yarn, gauge ranges, and recommended needle and hook sizes

Yarn weight category and symbol	0 LACE	1 SUPER FINE	2 FINE	3 LIGHT	4 MEDIUM	5 BULKY	6 SUPER BULKY
Types of Yarn in Category	Fingering 10-count crochet thread	Fingering, Sock, Baby	Sport, Baby	DK, Light Worsted	Worsted, Afghan, Aran	Chunky, Craft, Rug	Bulky, Roving
Knit Gauge Range in Stockinette stitch to 4 inches	33 – 40 stitches	27 – 32 stitches	23 – 26 stitches	21 – 24 stitches	16 – 20 stitches	12 – 15 stitches	6 –11 stitches
Recommended needle in metric size range	1.5 – 2.25 mm	2.25 – 3.25 mm	3.25 – 3.75 mm	3.75 – 4.5 mm	4.5 – 5.5 mm	5.5 – 8 mm	8 mm and Larger
Recommended needle in US size range	000 – 1	1 – 3	3 – 5	5 – 7	7 – 9	9 – 11	11 and Larger
Crochet Gauge* Range in single Crochet to 4 inches	32 – 42 double Crochet	21 – 32 stitches	16 – 20 stitches	12 – 17 stitches	11 – 14 stitches	8 – 11 stitches	5 – 9 stitches
Recommended Hook in metric size range	1.6 – 1.4 mm	2.25 – 3.5 mm	3.5 – 4.5 mm	4.5 – 5.5 mm	5.5 – 6.5 mm	6.5 – 9 mm	9 mm and Larger
Recommended Hook in US size range	6, 7, 8	B-1 to E-4	E-4 to 7	7 to I-9	I-9 to K-10 1/2	K-10 1/2 to M-13	M– 13 and Larger

The yarn weight is numbered on a scale from 00 to 6; 00 being the finest type of yarn and 6 being the thickest type of yarn. The chart also includes information like the recommended knitting needle size and hook size used for that type of yarn, and the gauge range (stitches per 4 inch knitted) using those needles. Keep in mind that the chart is only a guideline and the needle size, hook size and gauge is only commonly used for the type of yarn suggesting them.The chart also tells you some of the types of yarn in each category.

Chapter 2

Getting Started

What is Knitting?

There are three parts to a knitted piece:

1) **The cast on row**: The *cast on row* is the first row of stitches that makes up one edge of the fabric. This is done essentially by twisting the yarn into a loop and placing the loop onto a knitting needle. The simple twist action is what secures each stitch together so that the edge of the fabric does not unravel as you continue to knit. This process is repeated until the desired amount of stitches is on the first needle. The cast on row is what builds out the width of the fabric. The more stitches that are cast on, the wider the fabric will be.

2) **Working rows**: The *working rows* can be looked at as the "body" of the knitted fabric. It is the stitches that make up the fabric between the two edge rows. In the working rows, each stitch is worked by either knit or purl techniques. Each stitch interlocks with each other, but is not secured together, therefore if a stitch is missed or dropped off the needle, it can unravel the fabric by that one dropped stitch!

3) **The Bind off/Cast off row**: The *bind off* or also known as *cast off row*, is the last row of stitches and creates the other ending edge of the fabric. The bind off row, like the cast on row, secures the stitches together so that once the knitted fabric is complete; the stitches will not unravel.

How to Hold Knitting Needles

Knitting needles are held with the pointed end up and the capped end down. Hold the needle between your index finger and thumb. You want all the control of your needles to be with these two fingers. Next wrap your other three fingers around the needle below your thumb and index finger. These fingers provide support so that the needle doesn't move out of control. You don't need to grip your needle firmly with the last three.

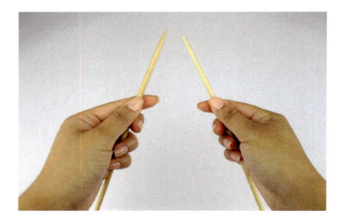

How To Hold Yarn

English Style

In English Style knitting, the yarn is held in the same hand as the working needle. This will be the style we use in this book. The yarn is wrapped around the working needle counter-clockwise to make a new stitch.

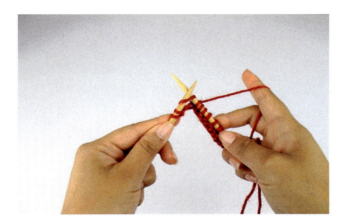

Continental Style

In continental style knitting the yarn is held with the same hand as the Holding needle. In Continental Knitting, the yarn is picked up by the working needle instead of the yarn being wrapped around.

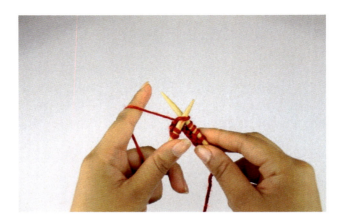

Left Handed Knitting

Most knitters use their right hand as the dominant knitting hand, but this can become really challenging if you are left hand dominant. Every knitting technique can be reversed and the left hand can be used as the dominant knitting hand.

Chapter 3

Casting on

How To Make a Slip Knot

A slip knot is the very first stitch on the needle. In order to get any stitches on the needles and start knitting you will need to make a slip knot. Here is a very easy way to make a slip knot.

1. Leaving about 2 ft of a yarn tail, hold the yarn between your index finger and thumb (your pinching fingers). Hold the yarn up so that as the yarn is folded, the two yarn strands are hanging straight down with the yarn tail on the right

2. Give the two strands a twist to the right, forming a loop where your index finger and thumb is holding the yarn.

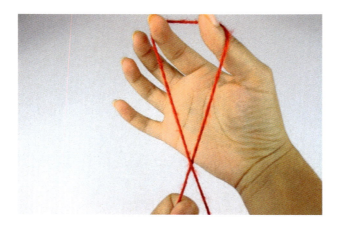

3. Take the left strand and pull it through the loop you made between your index and thumb. You have made a new loop which is the first stitch. Place the stitch on the knitting needle.

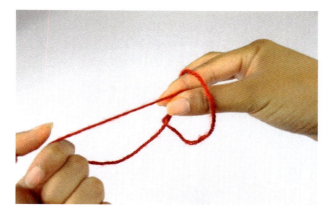

One-Needle Cast On

This method of Cast on is done using only one needle. In order to create a long tail cast on row, you will need a long tail of yarn since the stitches are made by both the tail yarn and the working yarn. You will need about 1 to 2 inches of yarn for every cast on stitch you make (depending on your needle size.) For small needles (2mm to 5 mm) use **1 inch / 1 stitch** ratio. For medium size needles (6mm to 9mm) use the **1.5 inch / 1 stitch** ratio. For bigger needles you can use 2 inch to 1 stitch or to be safe you can use **3 inch / 1 stitch** ratios. In this demonstration we will cast on 20 stitches. Have a tail of at least 20 inches before you make your slip knot. It is always better to have a longer tail than to have not enough.

(RIGHT handed/LEFT handed)

1. Hold the needle with the slip knot in your **RIGHT/LEFT** hand. Take both the tail end of the yarn and the working yarn and hold them together with your left hand.

2. Insert your left thumb and index finger in between the two yarns making sure the yarn touching your thumb is the tail end and the yarn by your index finger is the working yarn.

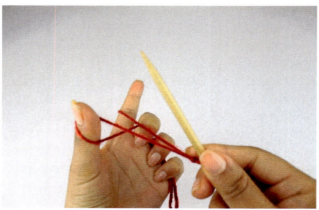

3. Lift your thumb and finger up so that you have one yarn strand wrapped around your thumb and one strand wrapped around your finger.

4. Insert the needle in to the loop on your thumb through the bottom.

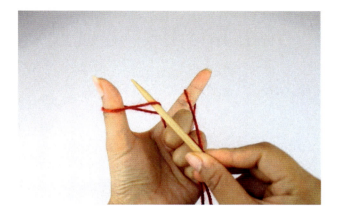

5. Keeping the needle through the loop on your thumb, insert the needle in the loop on your index finger through the top.

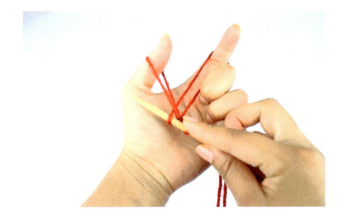

6. Pull the loop from your index finger through the loop on your thumb. Drop the loop off your thumb and pull to tighten. Then pick up the yarn again with your thumb.

7. Repeat these steps until you have the desired amount of cast on stitches on the needle.

Two needle Cast On

(RIGHT handed/LEFT handed)

1. Holding the needle with the slip knot in your **LEFT HAND**/**RIGHT HAND**, separate the two ends of the yarn so that you are not knitting with the tail end of the yarn but the end that is connected to the ball of yarn.

2. Bring the working yarn to the back of the needle so that it is pulled away from you instead of towards you.

3. Insert the working needle into the first stitch from **RIGHT to LEFT**/**LEFT to RIGHT** behind the holding needle; creating an "X" with the needles.

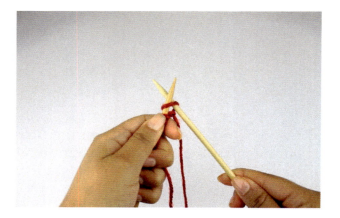

4. Wrap the working yarn **COUNTER-**

CLOCKWISE/**CLOCKWISE** around just the working needle so that the ends up between the two needles in the front.

5. using the working needle pull the yarn (that was wrapped around the needle) down and through the first stitch. There is now a new stitch on the working needle.

6. Place this new stitch back onto the holding needle by inserting the holding needle through the BOTTOM of the stitch that you just made on the working needle. There should now be two cast-on stitches on the holding needle.

7. Repeat these steps until you have the desired amount of stitches on the needle.

Chapter 4

The Two Basic Stitches

The Knit Stitch

Now that you have casted on stitches, we are going to begin with the first basic stitch, the **Knit Stitch**. The Knit stitch is one of the two basic types of stitches in knitting.

(Right handed/Left handed)

1. Making sure that the working yarn is to the back, insert the working needle into the first stitch on the holding needle from **RIGHT** to **LEFT**/**LEFT** to **RIGHT**, from the bottom of the stitch. The working needle crosses behind the holding needle.

2. Using your **LEFT**/**RIGHT** hand to hold both the

needles, wrap the working yarn around **COUNTERCLOCKWISE**/**CLOCKWISE** around the working needle. The yarn ends up between the two needles in the front.

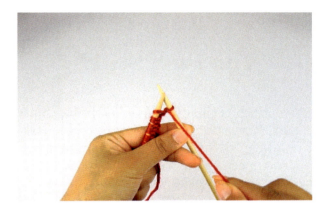

3. Using the working needle, pull the yarn through the stitch. There is now a new stitch forming on the working needle. Slide the old stitch on the holding needle completely off the needle. The new stitch is now on the working needle.

Slide this stitch off the needle.

4. Continue these steps for the rest of the stitches until all the new stitches are moved onto the working

needle.

Once all the stitches are on the working needle, the working needle will become the holding needle for the next row.

The Purl Stitch

The Purl stitch is the other basic stitch. You will come to see that **the Purl stitch is an inverted knit stitch**. On a knitted fabric, a Knit stitch on the right side of the fabric (the side that is shown outward on the fabric) will appear as a Purl stitch on the wrong side and a Purl stitch on the right side will appear as a Knit stitch.

(Right handed/Left handed)

1. Making sure that the working yarn is turned to the front of the needle (opposite than starting a knit stitch.) Insert the working needle into the first stitch on the holding needle from **RIGHT to LEFT**/**LEFT to RIGHT** through the top of the stitch. The working needle crosses in front of the holding needle

2. Wrap the yarn **COUNTERCLOCKWISE**
    /CLOCKWISE around the working needle. The
    yarn ends up between the two needles

3. With the working needle, pull the yarn through the stitch. The new stitch is now forming on the working needle

4. Slide the old stitch on the holding needle completely off the needle. The new stitch is now on the working needle.

5. Continue these steps for the rest of the stitches until all the new stitches are on the working needle. The working needle will now become the holding needle for the next row.

Since the Purl stitch and the Knit stitch are essentially the same stitch, purling all the stitches for every row will also create the Garter stitch pattern.

Transitioning from Knit to Purl Stitch

There are a lot more Stitch Patterns that are made from these two stitches. Many of them alternate from knit to purl and purl to knit stitches within the rows, so it is important to know how to properly transition between the two stitches in the pattern.

When moving from a Knit stitch to a Purl stitch simply move the working yarn to the front of the stitch by rotating the yarn counterclockwise (clockwise for left handed) to the front. This is called **Yarn Forward.**

Before a purl stitch.

When transitioning from a Purl stitch to a Knit stitch move the yarn to the back of the needle by rotating the yarn clockwise (counterclockwise for left handed.) This is called **Yarn Back**.

Before a knit stitch.

Chapter 5

Stitch Patterns

The Garter Stitch

The Garter Stitch pattern is a knitted fabric pattern that is made up of only Knit stitches or Purl stitches (you will learn the Purl stitch in next lesson). After knitting or purling all the stitches in the row, switch the needles around (working needle becomes the holding needle and holding needle becomes the working needle).

Garter Stitch pattern:

Knit or Purl every row

Stockinette Stitch Pattern

  The stockinette stitch is a stitch pattern that is made up of both knit stitch and purl stitches. Each row alternates Knit stitches for one row and and purl stitches for the next row. The stockinette stitch is one of the most popular stitch pattern as the knitting gauge is measured on stockinette fabric. This is the stockinette pattern.

Stockinette Stitch

Row 1: Knit all stitches

Row 2: Purl all stitches

These 2 rows form the pattern

Rib Stitch Pattern

1x1 rib Stitch Pattern:
Pattern Note:
Work each stitch in the manner it presents – *If you Knitted the stitch in one row, it will present as an Purl stitch in the following row. If the stitch was purled in the row, it will present as a knit stitch in the following row. Therefore, you would Knit the stitch if it was Purled in the previous row, and Purl the stitch if it was Knitted in the previous row.*

Row 1: *Knit 1 stitch, Purl 1 stitch* repeat pattern from * to * to last stitch in the row.

Row 2: Work each stitch in the manner it presents.
These 2 rows form the pattern

Seed Stitch Pattern

Seed Stitch Pattern
Pattern Note:
Work each stitch opposite to the manner it presents – *Knit the stitch if it was Knitted in the previous row, Purl the stitches if it was Purled in the previous row.*

Row 1: *Knit 1, Purl 1* repeat from * to * to last stitch

Row 2: Work each stitch opposite to the manner it presents.

These 2 rows form pattern

Chapter 6

Binding Off

Bind Off

The final row of your knitted piece is called the Bind off row. Like the Cast on row, the Bind off row seals the edge of the knitted fabric so that it does not unravel when the yarn is cut from the knitted piece. Binding off simply secures each stitch in the last row.

1. Work 2 stitches.

2. Lift the first stitch up and move it over and passed the second.

3. Drop the stitch off the needle. There should be only one stitch on your working needle

4. Work the next stitch, and then pass the previous stitch over that stitch and off the needle. Continue to work the row in this pattern.

5. When you get to the last stitch you can cut the yarn leaving a few inches but don't remove the knitting needle from the stitch. Then using the knitting needle pull on the stitch a little bit to make it bigger. Thread the last bit of the yarn through the stitch and

pull to secure.

Note* Work the stitches in pattern as you bind them off.

Example:

 binding off a rib stitch pattern:

1)k1, p1, bind off first stitch
2) k1, bind off first stitch
3) p1, bind off first stitch
4) k1, bind off first stitch
5) p1, bind off first stitch

Continue to last stitch.

Chapter 7

Basic Pattern Abbreviations

[ ] = work instructions between brackets, as many times as directed.
* = repeat instructions after asterisk
** = repeat instructions between asterisks

The brackets and asterisk are used in the pattern to tell you where to start a stitch or stitch pattern. In most patterns there is an edge stitch to start the row or end the row in order to create a nicely refined edge in your knitting. In this case the row will be read as:Row 1: K1 *K1, P1* K1 *(Knit 1 stitch for edge stitch, Repeat the pattern between the asterisk as Knit 1, Purl 1, end row with Knit 1 for edge stitch)*

CO = Cast On
BO = Bind Off
The pattern instructions will start and end with a Cast on row and Bind off row.

k= knit
p = purl
Usually for knitting and purling, the K or P abbreviation will have a number next to them like K1, P1. This means knit 1 stitch, purl 1 stitch. The pattern will say how many knit stitches to knit and purl stitches to purl.

RS = right side: The side of work that will be shown.
WS = wrong side; The side of work that won't be shown.
The right side of clothing fabric is the side that will be worn outside. The wrong side is the side that will be worn inside. (picture)

ss; sl st = slip a stitch
k-wise = knit-wise: Insert right needle into the stitch as if to knit it
p-wise = purl wise: Insert needle into stitch as though to purl it
When slipping stitches the pattern may indicate which way to insert the needle into the stitch to slip it. If a pattern does not indicate which way to slip the stitch, Slip the stitch p-wise on Knit stitches and k-wise on Purl stitches. (picture)

k2tog = knit 2 stitches together
p2tog = purl 2 together
psso = pass the slipped stitch over: After slipping stitch, Knit/Purl 1 and then pass the slipped stitch over the new stitch.
Wyib; yb= with yarn in back or yarn back
wyif; yf= with yarn in front or yarn forwardyo = yarn over: wrap the yarn once counterclockwise around working needle

pm = place marker
A marker is placed on the needle when there is a change in the pattern, can be used to count stitches, and used when knitting in the round and the marker indicates the beginning of the row.
When knitting with markers, knit the stitches the way the

pattern tells you to, and slip the markers when you come across them.

Edge Stitches

An edge stitch is also known as the selvage edge of the knitting fabric. In order to create a neater, finished edge, most stitch patterns offer an edge stitch. There are many different kinds of edge stitches but one of the most common is the garter stitch edge. This is where the first stitch and last stitch of every row is a knit stitch. The stitch pattern would ask that you cast on 2 extra stitches so that there can be an edge stitch on both sides of the fabric.

Chapter 8

Knitting Gauge

How to Measure Knitting Gauge

The knitting gauge is the amount of stitches it takes to make up every 4 inches (10 cm) of fabric. It is usually two measurements; how many stitches across per 4 inches, and how many rows per 4 inch of fabric.

The knitting gauge is best measured with fabric knitted in Stockinette Pattern.

You will need either a knitting gauge ruler or a regular ruler that is at least 4 inches long. Place your fabric onto a flat surface and flatten out the fabric so that it isn't curled.

Once you have your fabric flattened out, place your ruler across on the fabric with the first tic of the ruler lined up with the first stitch you are going to measure. A good tip would be to start measuring with a stitch that is a few over from the edge stitch. Once your ruler is lined up with the first stitch start counting how many stitches make up a full inch of the ruler across and down.

Multiply that number by 4 and you will get the knitting gauge of your fabric.

There are approximately 4 stitches per inch in this knitted fabric (it is about half a stitch under 1 inch)

There are approximately 7 rows per inch in this knitted fabric.

The knitting gauge is therefore 16 stitches and 28 rows per 4 inches

Fixing a Knitting Gauge

If you have more stitches in your knitting gauge than in the pattern's gauge:

This may mean that you are a tight knitter. Your stitches are then more close together than the knitter who made the pattern. You can either try knitting more loosely by not holding your yarn so tight when knitting or change your needle to one size bigger than the pattern's recommended needle size. You can keep the same tension as you did when you knitted your swatch of fabric, but because the needles are slightly bigger, your stitches will be more spaced out. Re-measure your knitting gauge until you have the same gauge as the pattern.

If you have less stitches in your knitting gauge than in the pattern's gauge:

This may mean that you are a loose knitter. Your stitches are then more spaced apart than the knitter who made the pattern. Just like the method above you can either fix the problem two different ways. If you only have a few stitches less than the patterns gauge, you can try to knit more tightly by keeping more tension when you hold your yarn and then re-measure your knitting gauge or change your needles to one size smaller than recommended in the pattern. You can keep the same tension as you did when you knitted your swatch of fabric, but because the needles are smaller your stitches will be knitted more close together. Re-measure your knitting gauge until you have the same gauge as the pattern.

Chapter 9

Basic Troubleshooting Techniques

Fixing a Dropped Stitch

1. Work stitches until you get to where the dropped stitch should be. Then turn your work so that the knit side is facing you.

2. Take an extra needle or crochet hook and reach through the dropped stitch to fish the bar behind it through the dropped stitch.

Using the extra needle, pull this bar down and through the dropped stitch

*A good tip is to use this needle to lift the dropped stitch up so that you can pull the bar stitch through with the extra needle, just like passing the first stitch over when binding off.

3. Once that stitch is pulled through, continue to pull the missed stitches from each row through until you get to the top.

Continue to pull each bar through each
dropped stitch until you get to the top

Un-Doing Stitches

1. Insert the **left**/**right** needle into the stitch under the
worked stitch on the working needle, from left to
right.

2. Slide the working needle out of the stitch. Don't
worry, the stitch will not be a dropped stitch because
the other needle is securing it. Continue to undo

stitches until you've reached the desired spot in your knitting.

Slide this stitch off the needle.

Accidentally Added Stitches

If your yarn is at the front before you knit, or to the back before you purl, it will look like there is an extra stitch on the needle.

If you notice the stitch right away, you can undo stitches and re-work the stitch correctly.

Stitch was knitted with the yarn in front.
There is now a double stitch.

Extra Edge Stitch

Quite often you'll notice that there appears to be an extra edge stitch when knitting. It all has to do with the yarn positioning. Simply move the yarn to the front or back, depending on the direction the stitch untwists.

Pull working yarn back and the extra stitch disappears.

Conclusion

Congratulations! You can now call yourself a knitter! Hopefully with all the techniques and information in this book, you are confident enough to start exploring more projects and expanding yourself in the knitting world! The journey has just begun and there are so many projects to be made and many projects to be created.

If you would like to learn more about knitting and would like to check out some of my awesome knitting tutorials, head on over to my website:

http://reshmabalkaran.com

I look forward to continue helping you along on your journey to becoming a Pro Knitter!

Sincerely,
Reshma Balkaran

Glossary

[ ] = work instructions between brackets, as many times as directed

* = repeat instructions after asterisk

* * = repeat instructions between asterisks

alt = alternate : usually directed after finishing a row, working the stitches
opposite to what they present. Knit when it presents a purl stitch. Purl when it presents a knit stitch.

approx = Approximately

Beg = Begin or Beginning

bet = Between

BO = Bind Off

CC = Contrasting Colour

cdd = Centred Double Decrease: Slip 2 together, knit 1, pass the slipped stitches over together

cm = Centimetre(s)

cn = Cable needle

CO = Cast On

cont = Continue

dec(s) = decrease(s)

dpn = Double pointed needles

EOR = end of row

foll = follow(s); following

g = gram(s)

inc(s) = increase(s)

k= knit

k tbl; K1 tbl; K1b = Knit stitch through the back loop (page . . .)

k-wise = knit-wise: Insert right needle into the stitch as if to knit it

k2tog = knit 2 stitches together

m = Meter(s)

mm = millimeter(s)

MC = Main Colour
M1 = Make 1: Increase a stitch. If the method isn't specified, you can increase a stitch however you like.
oz = ounce(s)
p = purl
pat = pattern(s)
p tbl; P1 tbl; P1b = purl through the back loop
p-wise = purl wise: Insert needle into stitch as though to purl
p2tog = purl 2 together
pm = place marker
psso = pass the slipped stitch over: After slipping stitch, Knit/Purl 1 and then pass the slipped stitch over the new stitch.
pu = pick up stitches: After a knitted piece has already been Binded off, you can always add more length along an edge by picking up stitches with a new ball of yarn.
rem = remain(s)(ing)
Rep = repeat
RS = right side: The side of work that will be shown. For example, knitted clothing, the right side would be the side that is worn outside to be shown.
rnd(s) = round(s)
SKP; skpo = Slip 1 stitch, knit the next stitch, pass the slipped stitch over the knitted stitch. Can also be read as sl1, k1, psso
Sk2P = slip1, knit 2 together, pass the slipped stitch over: Double decrease
S2KP = Slip 2 stitches, knit 1, pass the slipped stitches over the knitted stitch
ss; sl st = slip a stitch
sl 1 k-wise = slip a stitch knit-wise
sl 1 p-wise = slip a stitch purl-wise
ssk = slip 2 stitches, knit the slipped stitches together(decrease)
sssk = Slip 3 stitches, knit the 3 slipped stitches together (double decrease)

st (s) = stitch(es)
tbl = through the back loop
tog = together
WS = wrong side; The side of work that won't be shown. For example, knitted clothing, the right side would be the side that is worn inside, not to be shown.
Wyib = with yarn in back
wyif = with yarn in front
yo = yarn over: wrap the yarn around working needle

About the Author

"Everyone is an artist, everyone is creative, but most people don't know it. Either they haven't found their art yet, or they haven't given themselves the chance to find it. I'm determined to help people find the creativity within themselves." - Reshma Balkaran

Reshma Balkaran is a DIY fanatic! She has dedicated her life to creating beautiful and fashionable do-it-yourself crafts, home décor art and clothing in which she teaches and shares with the rest of the world with her blog, video tutorials and books.

With a background in Dance, Reshma found her passion for at home DIY art projects when she decided to start making her own dance costumes due to her low budget lifestyle. She spent most of her days designing, sewing, stitching and crafting up new pieces. The joy and pride that she found knowing that you can create so openly encouraged her to share her knowledge with the world, and build a community of artists wanting to share their own creative ideas!

In her spare time, she loves to knit, draw, paint, sew and craft as many things as she can and enjoys sharing them all through her blog and videos.

To find out what she is working on next, visit

www.ReshmaBalkaran.com.

Manufactured by Amazon.ca
Bolton, ON